# 12 WOMEN IN EDUCATION

by Marne Ventura

12 STORY LIBRARY
MORE TO EXPLORE

www.12StoryLibrary.com



12-Story Library is an imprint of Bookstaves.

Photographs ©: US Congress/PD, cover, 1; Hans Dunkelberg der Jüngere/PD, 4; Library of Congress, 5; WENN Rights Ltd/Alamy, 6; SPGOALS TV/YouTube, 7; Jack de Nijs/Anefo/PD, 7; Shawn Miller/Library of Congress, 8; Shawn Miller/Library of Congress, 9; PD, 10; FOTO:FORTEPAN/Juli/CC3.0, 11; Library of Congress, 12; Boston Public Library/CC2.0, 13; PD, 13; PD, 14; Ontario Ministry of Education/PD, 15; Simon Davis/DFID/CC2.0, 16; Matt Dunham/Associated Press, 17; PD, 18; NSW State Archives/PD, 19; PD, 19; Addison Scurlock/CC2.0, 20; Florida Memory/PD, 21; PD, 21; Agence de presse Meurisse/PD, 22; Associated Press, 23; US Congress/PD, 24; John Rous/Associated Press, 25; Monika Flueckiger/World Economic Forum/CC2.0, 26; Roger L. Wollenberg/UPI/Newscom, 27; Pandita Ramabai Sarasvati/PD, 28; Library of Congress, 29

**ISBN**
9781632357755 (hardcover)
9781632358844 (paperback)
9781645820550 (ebook)

**Library of Congress Control Number: 2019938625**

Printed in the United States of America
September 2019

About the Cover
Patsy Mink in the 1970s.

Access free, up-to-date content on this topic plus a full digital version of this book. Scan the QR code on page 31 or use your school's login at 12StoryLibrary.com.

# Table of Contents

# 1 Anne Sullivan: Students with Disabilities Can Learn

Anne Sullivan was the teacher and lifelong friend of Helen Keller. She was born Johanna Mansfield Sullivan in 1866 in Massachusetts. But everyone called her Anne or Annie. An eye disease at age five left her nearly blind. Her mother died when Sullivan was eight. Two years later, her father left her at a home for poor people. Sullivan wanted to get an education and make a better life for herself. She asked to go to school. She was sent to a special school for the blind in Boston. She had surgery on her eyes. It improved her vision enough to read.

Anne Sullivan circa 1887.

In 1886, Sullivan graduated at the top of her class. She took a job as a tutor for seven-year-old Helen Keller, who was deaf and blind. Sullivan tried a new way of reaching Keller. She traced letters onto Keller's hand to spell out words. In six months, Keller learned 575 words and could do math.

Sullivan stayed with Helen for the rest of her life. First Helen went to the special school for the blind where Anne had gone. Then she went to Radcliffe College. Sullivan spelled out the lectures to her and helped her

Sullivan (right) with Helen Keller.

read and study. After graduation, Sullivan and Keller traveled around the world and gave lectures. They showed that people without sight, hearing, and speech can be educated and make a contribution to the world.

## 14

**Anne Sullivan's age when she entered Perkins School for the Blind**

- Sullivan couldn't read or write when she started school.
- She learned to use the manual alphabet to communicate with a friend who was deaf and blind.
- She later used this skill to teach Helen Keller.

### THINK ABOUT IT

Anne Sullivan overcame many obstacles to get an education. Why do you think she was so determined to go to school?

# 2

# Buffy Sainte-Marie: Champion for Native People

Buffy Sainte-Marie receiving the Lifetime Contribution to Aboriginal Music Award in 2008.

Buffy Sainte-Marie was born Beverly Sainte-Marie in 1941. She was born on a Cree reservation in Saskatchewan, Canada. Her parents died when she was a baby. Family members who lived in Massachusetts adopted her. As a child, she taught herself to play piano and guitar. She studied teaching in college.

Sainte-Marie became a singer-songwriter. She sang about civil rights and against war. By the time she was 24, she earned enough money to live comfortably. She began to work to help Native Americans.

In 1969, she started a foundation called Nihewan. It helps Native students get to college.

**$0.00**

**What it cost students and teachers to use the Cradleboard project**

- From 1996 to 2009, Sainte-Marie wrote a series of lesson plans.
- The lessons taught Native American culture for grades 3–12.
- Sainte-Marie paid for the project with donations and her own money.

## SESAME STREET

From 1976 to 1981, Buffy Sainte-Marie was a guest on the children's TV show *Sesame Street*. She taught children that Native Americans are still around, not a thing of the past. She talked and sang songs to other characters on the show. She encouraged pride in diverse cultures.

Students can apply for scholarships. Two scholarship winners have gone on to start their own tribal colleges. Sainte-Marie is especially proud of that.

In 1997, Sainte-Marie founded the Cradleboard Teaching Project. She wanted to help students learn about Native American culture and history. She created a website. It had lesson plans and information about Native people around the world. The project ran for 12 years. Sainte-Marie hopes to restart it in the near future.

Sainte-Marie playing her mouthbow in 1968.

# 3

# Carla Hayden: First Woman Librarian of Congress

Carla Hayden was born in 1952. She grew up in Chicago. As a child, she loved reading and libraries. She began her career as a librarian in 1973. Her first job was at the Chicago Public Library. Then she worked at Chicago's Museum of Science and Industry.

Hayden earned her PhD in Library Science in 1987 from the University of Chicago. After that, she taught at the University of Pittsburgh. In 1993, she became director of Enoch Pratt Free Library in Baltimore. She spent the next 23 years there.

Carla Hayden in 2018.

In all of her jobs, Hayden made her work about public service. At the Pratt, she started an outreach program for teens. They could come to the library for homework help. They could get help with applying to college and choosing a career.

Hayden says that libraries are the cornerstones of democracy. They are places where information is free and available to everyone. She

Hayden reading to children.

sees librarians as activists, social workers, and fighters for freedom.

On February 24, 2016, President Barack Obama chose Hayden to be the 14th Librarian of Congress. She was the first African American picked for the job. She was also the first woman.

## THINK ABOUT IT

In America, libraries are free. In some countries, this isn't true. Why are libraries so important to democracy?

## 2018

**Year when Carla Hayden won the Newberry Library Award**

- Hayden was honored for her service to the public as a librarian.
- She has fought for all Americans to have free access to information.
- She has been a leader in using technology in libraries.

# 4 Ella Flagg Young: First Female School Superintendent

Ella Flagg Young was an American educator. She was born in New York in 1845. Her parents didn't send her to school as a child, so she taught herself to read and write. When she was 15, she passed a teachers' exam. But she was told she was too young to be hired. In 1862, she graduated from Chicago Normal School and became a teacher.

Young gave her life to teaching. She taught primary school and high school. She taught education at the University of Chicago. She became principal of the Chicago Normal School. From 1909–1915, she was superintendent of Chicago schools. This was the first time a woman was in charge of a big-city school system in the United States.

Meanwhile, Chicago was in a period of change. The Industrial Revolution had created many new jobs. Schools and classrooms became more diverse. Young worked to give teachers better training. She gave

Ella Flagg Young in 1916.

them more say in how their programs were run. She fought for better pay for teachers. She added counselors to schools to help students in need of advice.

## WOMEN'S MOVEMENT

Ella Flagg Young was also a key player in the Women's Movement. While she was head of Chicago schools, women activists were fighting for equal rights. Young worked to help these groups. Leaders of the movement saw her as a role model. She was a symbol of success.

**53**

**Number of years Ella Flagg Young worked in education**

- Young ran Chicago's public schools as a democracy.
- She gave teachers more power to make decisions about their work.
- She was also the first woman president of the National Education Association.

# 5 Harriet Beecher Stowe: Writing Against Slavery

Harriet Beecher Stowe circa 1880.

Harriet Beecher Stowe was an American writer. She was born in Litchfield, Connecticut, in 1811. She was from a religious, well-educated family. Harriet and her husband were against slavery. They helped enslaved people who were fleeing the South.

In 1850, the US Congress passed a law. It made it illegal to help enslaved people escape. Stowe used her writing skills to raise awareness about slavery. Her novel, *Uncle Tom's Cabin*, came out a chapter at a time in a national newspaper. In 1852, it was published as a book. It became a best seller.

*Uncle Tom's Cabin* tells the story of Tom, an elderly enslaved man.

**300,000**

**Copies of *Uncle Tom's Cabin* sold in the year after it was printed**

- The book came out in 1852, about a year after the Civil War began.
- President Lincoln joked that Stowe started the war by writing the book.
- *Uncle Tom's Cabin* was the best-selling novel of the 19th century.

The novel describes the hardships of slavery. Slave traders sell people. Families are separated. Enslaved people are beaten and often killed. Stowe's writing raised the North's awareness about how enslaved people were treated. It showed the point of view of Americans who wanted an end to slavery.

## THE REAL-LIFE UNCLE TOM

Stowe based her main character on a formerly enslaved man named Josiah Henson. Henson was born in Maryland in 1789. As a child, he was separated from his parents and treated cruelly. As a young man, he escaped to Canada with his wife and children. From Canada, Henson helped enslaved Americans escape to freedom. In 1849, Henson met Stowe and told her his story.

# 6 Lucy Wheelock: Bringing Kindergarten into Schools

Lucy Wheelock circa 1893.

Lucy Wheelock was an American teacher. She was born in 1857 in Vermont. After high school, she studied education for very young children. She learned from some of the leading educators of the time.

Wheelock taught kindergarten in a private school for 10 years. Then she trained other teachers. In 1888, Boston Public Schools added kindergartens to their schools for the first time. Wheelock created the Wheelock Training School to prepare teachers. She also headed a Sunday school in Boston. She trained Sunday school teachers to use the same methods used in kindergartens. She gave lectures about education. She wrote articles for teachers about early learning.

Kindergarten began as a system for teaching young children through play. A German teacher named Friedrich Froebel created it in 1837. The first kindergartens in the United States were opened in 1860. Through her work with kindergartens, Wheelock raised awareness about the importance of school for the very young. She believed that good preschools and kindergartens helped fight poverty. Poor children who start early often stay in school longer. Many also get better jobs as adults.

Student teachers practice teaching kindergarten in 1898.

## KINDERGARTEN

Friedrich Froebel coined the word kindergarten. It's from the German words that mean "children" and "garden." His system used music, nature study, stories, and play to teach young children. He came up with the idea of children sitting in a circle to learn. He stressed the use of crafts.

**1859**

**Year when Lucy Wheelock started a free kindergarten**

- The kindergarten was at Hope Chapel in Boston.
- Later, Wheelock founded a second at South End House in Boston.
- Her goal was to make sure poor children got early education.

# 7

# Malala Yousafzai: Educating Girls in Pakistan

Malala Yousafzai in 2015.

Malala Yousafzai is a Pakistani activist for female education. She is also the youngest-ever winner of the Nobel Prize. Yousafzai was born in 1997 in Pakistan. Her father ran a chain of schools. He believed in education for all children. Yousafzai's father taught her to read and write at a young age. He encouraged her to become active in politics. She was a good student and loved learning.

When Yousafzai was 11, the local Taliban banned girls in her area from going to school. Yousafzai began writing a blog for the British Broadcasting Company (BBC). It described her life under the Taliban occupation. She used a pen name to avoid putting herself in danger. She knew the Taliban would be angry about her writing. But after she appeared on TV shows, her identity was no longer a secret. To silence Yousafzai, a Taliban gunman shot her in the head. She was 15 years old at the time.

Yousafzai survived the shooting. She had many surgeries over the next months. After her recovery, she continued to fight for education

**17**

**Malala Yousafzai's age when she won the Nobel Peace Prize**

- Her shooting raised awareness for girls' education in Pakistan.
- Soon after, Pakistani officials ratified the first Right to Education Bill.
- Yousafzai speaks around the world in support of education for all children.

## TALIBAN

The Taliban is a military religious group. It controlled most of Afghanistan and parts of Pakistan during the late 1990s. It was first made up of students who were trained in Islamic religious schools in Pakistan. The Taliban excludes women from public life. Women aren't allowed to have jobs or go to school.

rights. She founded the Malala Fund to help promote education. She wrote a best-selling book about her experience. In 2014, she was awarded the Nobel Peace Prize.

Yousafzai accepting the Nobel Peace Prize.

8

# Maria Montessori: Letting Children Choose

Maria Montessori was an Italian doctor and teacher. She invented the Montessori method of early childhood education. Born in Italy in 1870, she started school when she was six years old. She was a good science and math student. After high school, she studied medicine. She was one of the first women to receive a Doctor of Medicine degree from the University of Rome. She began working with children with mental disabilities.

Montessori learned as much as she could about teaching children with disabilities. She read all the experts. She gave talks at teacher training schools. She urged schools to offer special classes for the disabled. She also spoke up for special training for teachers. In 1900, she became co-director of a school for the disabled. People thought these children couldn't learn. Montessori showed they could be taught.

In 1901, Montessori started studying for another degree at the University of Rome. She began to develop a method to teach children without disabilities. She based it on the same system that worked so well with children who were disabled. In 1907, she opened a school for two- to seven-year-olds. It was called Casa dei Bambini, for Children's House. Children got to choose their

A Montessori classroom in 1913.

activities. They often chose cleaning, dusting, working with clay, or caring for plants and animals. The children worked with special learning materials Montessori designed. Students who went through her program became more independent. They had better concentration and more self-discipline.

**22,000**

**Estimated number of Montessori schools worldwide today**

- The first Montessori school in the United States opened in 1911.
- A book Montessori wrote to describe her method became a best seller.
- By 1913, there were more than 100 Montessori schools in the United States.

# 9

# Mary McLeod Bethune: Educating African Americans

Mary McLeod Bethune circa 1930.

**$11**

**Monthly rent Mary McLeod Bethune paid for her first school in 1904**

- Her students were the children of poor black workers on the Florida railroad.
- Classes were held in a rundown building.
- Bethune used discarded barrels and crates for desks and chairs.

Mary McLeod Bethune was an African American educator and civil rights activist. She was born in 1875 in South Carolina. Her parents worked on the plantation where they had been enslaved. Bethune was the 15th of 17 children. Until she was 10, there was no school for blacks in her area. When one opened in 1885, Bethune walked five miles (8 km) each way to attend. She was the first member of her family to go to school.

After graduation, Bethune worked to give African Americans better opportunities for education. In 1904, she started a school for African

Bethune with her students in Florida circa 1905.

American girls in Florida. The school began with five girl students and

Bethune's son. The students and their families raised funds for the school by selling baked goods and handmade items. Bethune spoke to wealthy businessmen and asked for donations. The school slowly grew. In 1923, it merged with a boy's school. Today it is Bethune-Cookman College. Bethune was head of the college until 1942 and again from 1946–47.

In 1935, Bethune founded the National Council of Negro Women. This group worked to end segregation and discrimination. In 1936, she became director of Negro Affairs for the National Youth Administration. This group worked for social change, such as fair wages. It worked to help young African Americans succeed. Bethune became a friend to President Franklin Roosevelt and First Lady Eleanor Roosevelt. FDR chose her as a member of a cabinet of African American advisers. She spoke out for civil rights, voter rights, and better jobs for African Americans.

Bethune (left) with First Lady Eleanor Roosevelt (center) in 1943.

10

# Nadia Boulanger: Greatest Music Teacher

Nadia Boulanger (left) with her sister Lili in 1913.

Nadia Boulanger was a French musician and educator. Some say she was the greatest music teacher of all time. She was born Juliette Nadia Boulanger in 1887 in France. Her father taught voice lessons in Paris. Boulanger went to music school from the age of 10 until she was 17. She was a gifted student. She won many prizes in musical contests.

After graduation, she wrote and performed music. She also taught music composition. One of her students was her younger sister, Lili. At age 19, Lili won an important prize for a composition. She died when she was just 24. Lili had been sick since childhood. After her death, Boulanger gave up composing. She devoted herself to teaching.

Boulanger had many American students. Two were Aaron Copland and Quincy Jones. Both became very successful composers. Boulanger became famous for being a great teacher. She stressed traditional, academic music concepts. At the same time, she helped her students find their own special style.

Boulanger conducting in 1937.

Boulanger was the first woman to conduct the Royal Philharmonic Orchestra. This was in London in 1937. In 1938, she was the first woman to conduct the Boston Symphony Orchestra, the New York Philharmonic Orchestra, and the Philadelphia Orchestra.

## THINK ABOUT IT

One of her students described Boulanger as intimidating and terrifying. Boulanger insisted that her students work very hard. At the same time, she never tried to influence their individual style. Why do you think she is considered such a great teacher?

**1979**

**Year when Nadia Boulanger died at age 92**

- Until a few months before her death, she was still working with music students.
- She worked with all types of musicians.
- For much of her working life, she taught from 8 a.m. to 10 p.m.

# 11

# Patsy Mink: Women's Rights and Title IX

Patsy Mink in the 1970s.

Patsy Mink was the first Asian American woman elected to Congress. She was born Patsy Takemoto in Hawaii in 1927. In high school, she was the top student in her class. She earned two degrees in science from the University of Hawaii.

Then she applied to several medical schools. None would accept her because she was a woman. So she went to law school.

Mink went to the University of Chicago. She was the first Hawaiian woman to earn a law degree there. In 1951, she married and had a daughter. She applied for jobs at law firms. None would hire a woman with a young child. They felt she wouldn't be able to devote enough time to her work. So she decided to enter politics.

Mink returned to Hawaii and worked in local politics. In 1962, she was elected to Hawaii's state senate. She was head of the education committee. In 1964, she was elected to the US House of Representatives. She stayed in Congress for four decades. Mink worked to improve child care, bilingual education, and student loans. She worked to improve special education, working conditions for teachers, and early childhood education. She fought for equal rights for women in education and the workforce, and she was a strong advocate for the environment.

Mink is best known for her work on Title IX (1972). This law prohibited schools and programs that received money from the US government from discriminating on the basis of sex.

**13**

**Number of sessions Patsy Mink served in the US House of Representatives**

- Her Title IX law banned unequal treatment for men and women in education.
- Today more women than men attend college.
- Medical and law schools today are almost equal in numbers of male and female students.

Mink meeting with her Hawaii colleagues in Washington DC in 1966.

# 12 Susan Hockfield: MIT's First Woman President

Susan Hockfield at the World Economic Forum in 2012.

Born in Chicago in 1951, Susan Hockfield is an American neuroscientist. She graduated from the University of Rochester in New York with a degree in biology. She got her PhD from Georgetown University. She worked as a medical researcher. In 1985, she became a professor at Yale University. She stayed for 20 years. Some of her discoveries led to new ways to treat brain cancer. She helped create programs where researchers in different departments work together. She helped graduate programs get more money for their research, and student workers more pay.

In 2004, Massachusetts Institute of Technology asked Hockfield to be their president. MIT is world-famous for its research. It's best known for its work in physical sciences such as engineering. Hockfield was the first woman to head MIT. She was also the first biologist to take the job.

Hockfield headed MIT from 2004 to 2012. Under her leadership, MIT started a new program to develop better, cleaner energy sources. In 2011, President Barack Obama made Hockfield co-chair of a group

# $300 million

**Funding for Susan Hockfield's MIT Energy Initiative**

- Hockfield urged physical and life scientists to cooperate on solving energy problems.
- She set up the Koch Institute, where physical and life scientists work together on cancer research.
- She founded a Diversity Leadership Congress to help women and minority students in education.

## WHY SO FEW WOMEN?

In 2016, only 30 percent of American college presidents were women. Just 5 percent were women of color. Why? One reason is the people in charge of hiring college presidents are usually men. They don't have experience working with women leaders. So they don't feel comfortable hiring them.

that helped researchers work with government and industry leaders. She also helped create online learning materials for students around the world to use.

Hockfield joins President Barack Obama to promote investments in clean energy and new technology in 2009.

# Out of the Shadows

Pandita Ramabai in 1922.

## Pandita Ramabai

Ramabai was born in 1858 in India. Most Indian women at the time were not schooled. They were forced to marry at a young age. Ramabai fought for better conditions for women and children. She gave talks about women's rights. She set up a women's shelter and school.

## Huda Sha'arawi

When Sha'arawi was born in 1879, Egyptian women were confined to their homes. When and if they went out in public, they had to cover their faces. Sha'arawi fought for women's education. She set up a clinic for poor women. She fought for women's rights in politics and founded the Egyptian Feminist Union. As a protest, she uncovered her face in public.

## Savitrabai Phule

Phule was born in India in 1831, a time when Indian women had very few rights. She fought for their right to go to school. She set up India's first women's school that allowed poor people. She was the first woman teacher in India. She went on to build 18 more schools.

## Emma Willard

Willard was born in 1787 in Connecticut. Back then, men went to college and women went to finishing schools. Women were expected to marry and raise children. Willard founded the first school for women's higher education. More high schools and colleges for girls followed. Willard also wrote several textbooks.

A statue of Emma Willard in Troy, NY.

# Glossary

**activist**
A person who fights for social change.

**civil rights**
Human rights such as life and freedom.

**cornerstone**
An important building block of something.

**culture**
The social practices, beliefs, and ways of living of a group of people.

**disability**
The lack of ability to do something, such as see or hear.

**discrimination**
The unfair treatment of a group of people.

**diverse**
Different, such as from a different culture.

**Industrial Revolution**
A time during the late 1700s and early 1800s when the use of machines became widespread.

**outreach**
A program in education to help students in need.

**reservation**
An area of land set aside for Native Americans.

**segregation**
The separation of people based on sex, race, class, or age.

# Read More


Delano, Marfe Ferguson. *Helen's Eyes: A Photobiography of Annie Sullivan, Helen Keller's Teacher.* Washington, DC: National Geographic, 2015.

Barghoorn, Linda. *Buffy Sainte-Marie: Musician, Indigenous Icon, and Social Activist* Remarkable Lives Revealed. New York: Crabtree Publishing, 2018.

Schwartz, Heather E. *Mary McLeod Bethune: Education and Equality.* Huntington Beach, CA: Teacher Created Materials, 2017.

# Index



## About the Author

Marne Ventura has written over 80 books for children. A former elementary school teacher, she holds a master's degree in education from the University of California. Marne and her husband live on the central coast of California.